HEROES OF FAITH

Bob McDoniel

James Kay Publishing

Tulsa, Oklahoma

This work is intended to be an examination of the inspired account of examples of living faith recorded in Hebrews 11. The thoughts, suggestions, and comments are the result of the author's study.

Heroes of Faith
ISBN 978-1-943245-21-5

www.jameskaypublishing.com

e-mail: sales@jameskaypublishing.com

© 2018 Bob McDoniel
Cover design by JKP
Cover Photo & Author Photo by Dorothy McDoniel

All rights reserved.
No part of this book may be reproduced in any form or by any means without permission in writing from the author.

also by
Bob McDoniel.

Jeremiah
God's Messenger to an Antagonistic People

Scan to Order

Dedication

This book is dedicated to the
Eastside church
in Muskogee, Oklahoma
who encourage me
to keep studying.

Note:

The section of scripture which will be examined in this study is to be found in Hebrews 11:1-32. In order to get a full grasp of the case for faith presented in this chapter, it would be helpful to read this section of scripture in its entirety prior to studying the individual characters presented. As you get into the study of the individual Heroes of Faith you will notice that all scripture quotations are taken from the New King James version of the Bible and are typed in italics Other scripture references which aid in understanding these individuals will be printed in bold type. Although these passages are not written out, it is recommended that the student read them for himself to understand the people being examined more completely.

Robert McDoniel

Introduction

The writer of the Book of Hebrews was writing to a group of discouraged Jewish Christians. They were so discouraged they were in danger of giving up on Christianity and going back into the life and practice they had known under the Old Covenant. This being the case, the author presents arguments for remaining true to Christ and continuing on in spite of tribulations, hardships, and discouragement. The New Covenant had a greater High Priest, greater promises, a greater hope, a greater sacrifice, and was greater in scope than the Old Covenant had ever been. To remain true and steadfast in this covenant would require a strong, active faith.

The eleventh chapter of the book is devoted entirely to this subject of saving faith. The chapter begins with a definition that "faith is the substance of things hoped for and the evidence of things not seen" (Hebrews 11:1). Shortly after this beginning, the writer points to the necessity of possessing such a faith if one will be able to approach God and please him. Hebrews 11:6. After defining faith and pointing out the essentiality of having such a faith, the writer spends the majority of the chapter illustrating what this saving faith looks like. From the arguments made it becomes clear that we are talking about far more than the mental assent or belief that many think of when the subject of faith is mentioned. Truly, the picture of faith presented in this chapter might well be expressed with the equation: saving faith equals belief plus trust plus obedience or SF=B+T+O.

With this in mind, in this book we will attempt to look at these examples of saving faith individually so that we may determine how each of these heroes of faith demonstrated this vital element in their service to God.

The goal will be that after viewing this great cloud of witnesses individually, we also will be motivated to lay aside every weight and the sin which ensnares us and run with endurance the race set before us.

Contents

Introduction		xi
Abel	Hebrews 11:4	1
Enoch	Hebrews 11:5	5
Noah	Hebrews 11:7	11
Abraham	Hebrews 11:8-12, 17-19	17
Isaac	Hebrews 11:20	23
Jacob and Joseph	Hebrews 11:21,22	29
Moses	Hebrews 11:23-28	35
The Fall of Jericho and Rahab	Hebrews 11:29-31	41
Gideon	Hebrews 11:32	47
Barak	Hebrews 11:32	53
Samson	Hebrews 11:32	59
Jephthah	Hebrews 11:32	65
David	Hebrews 11:32	71
Samuel	Hebrews 11:32	77

ABEL

The first of the heroes listed by the Hebrews writer is Abel. The text reads: *"By faith Abel offered to God a more excellent sacrifice than Cain, through which he obtained witness that he was righteous, God testifying of his gifts; and through it he being dead still speaks." (Hebrews 11:4).*

Abel's story is recorded in **Genesis 4:1-12.** The Hebrews writer tells us that his sacrifice was by faith and was more excellent than Cain's. For this act to be by faith Abel must have somehow known what God desired in a sacrifice. At some point God must have communicated what he expected from his people when they offered sacrifices to him. Paul told the Romans that "faith comes by hearing, and hearing by the word of God" (Romans 10:17). The excellence of Abel's sacrifice is seen in the quality of the gift offered. Both men gave offerings of what they had. The difference I believe is seen in the attitude of the giver. "Cain brought an offering of the fruit of the ground to the LORD." Cain gave some. Abel, on the other hand, gave his best, "the firstborn of the flock and their fat." By giving the best he had, Abel would have been demonstrating greater respect and honor to God. Others have suggested that his sacrifice was more excellent in that he gave the greatest gift, the gift of life for the life is in the blood. **Genesis 9:3-5.** This may be the case. We only know that his sacrifice was more excellent and that his sacrifice was accepted by God while Cain's was not.

God has testified of Abel's righteousness through these scriptures which tell us of Abel and his approved sacrifice. It is through this scriptural witness of God that Abel speaks even though he has been dead for all of these centuries. **Genesis 4:4, 5.** Following the murder of his brother, which is recorded in **Genesis 4:8-9**, Cain was told that the blood of his brother cried out from the grave (Genesis 4:9). And in **Hebrews 12:24** we are told that the testimony of Jesus' blood speaks greater things than the blood of Abel.

To understand this, we must first determine what the blood of Abel says.

(1) One lesson from Abel might be that God will avenge the death of the righteous. That message is clearly taught in the New Testament in passages like **Romans 12:19**

and **Hebrews 10:30.** While it may appear for a time that the wicked prosper and go unpunished, a day of judgment and retribution is coming. This is brought out in **2 Corinthians 5:10** and **2 Thessalonians 1:6-9.** God certainly punished Cain for his actions.

(2) The blood of Abel also declares that the righteous will be hated without cause. Abel did not deserve to be killed by Cain. This lesson that the righteous will suffer without cause is also clearly taught in the New Testament. We find this message in **1 John 3:11-13; Matthew 5:10-12; 2 Timothy 3:12; John 15:18; and 1 Peter 3:13-17, 4:12-16.**

(3) A third message from the life of Abel is that it does make a difference how men worship. Some worship will be acceptable before God and other worship will be rejected. This was the case with Abel and Cain. In the New Testament we are told the only acceptable way to worship is the manner which God has commanded. **John 4:24; Mark 7:7;** and **2 John 9.** Faith is the key to acceptable worship. For *"that which is not of faith is sin..."* (Roman 14:28).

Questions on Abel:

1. How was Abel's sacrifice by faith?

2. How was Abel's sacrifice more excellent?

3. How has God testified of Abel's righteousness?

4. What does the blood of Abel say?

5. Discuss how Abel's actions demonstrate the "belief plus trust plus obedience" model.

Enoch

As little as we are told about Abel, we seem to know even less about the man we will study in this lesson, Enoch. We first read about this man in **Genesis 5:19-24.** From this section of scripture, we learn that Enoch was the son of Jared, the father of Methuselah, and walked with God 365 years on this earth. There is another Enoch mentioned In Genesis chapter four. That man was the son of Cain. The man we are looking at is a descendant of Seth. The Enoch of this lesson is the seventh in line from Adam and is the great-grandfather of Noah. **Genesis 5:4-29**. We can know that this is the Enoch the Hebrews writer is writing about because of what is said in the Hebrews passage about God taking him away or translating him. *"By faith Enoch was taken away so that he did not see death, and was not found, because God had taken him; for before he was taken he had this testimony, that he pleased God."* (Hebrews 11:5). We will come back to this matter of God taking Enoch away shortly.

Enoch stands out from the Patriarchs who went before him and those who came after him in some significant ways.

First, in a time when those around him were living well into their 900s, Enoch had only 365 years on this earth. His father lived to be 962 and his son lived to be 969.

Second, while the text says that all of these other men lived so many years after begetting their son, Genesis 5:22 says Enoch walked with God 300 years after begetting Methuselah. While these other men lived, Enoch walked with God. This alone speaks volumes about this man of faith.

One thing it tells us is that Enoch was in agreement with God. The prophet Amos writes, *"Can two walk together unless they are agreed?" (Amos 3:3).* The fact that Enoch walked with God says that Enoch was a man who cared about what the LORD requires of a man. **Micah 6:8.** This statement says that Enoch was seeking to be perfect as his father in heaven was perfect. Look at what John writes in **1 John 1:5-7.** Both verses 22 and 24 of Genesis 5 tell us that Enoch walked with God. George DeHoff suggests that this phrase, walked with God, indicates that Enoch lived a life of communion with God, obeying his word, seeking to honor his name.[1]

As a result of this life of dedication to God, God translated or took him. Enoch is one of only two men we read about in the Bible who never died. The other was the prophet Elijah. Imagine a life so totally dedicated to God that God would allow him to come be with him without having to first taste of death. That was the situation with Enoch. Enoch lived a life faithful to God in a world of which it will be said just three generations later that *"every intent of the thoughts of their heart was only evil continually" (Genesis 6:5).*

Enoch was one of only three men in all the Bible who were said to have walked with God. The other two were Noah and David. And unlike those others, nothing negative is said about Enoch's life. Before he was taken by God he had this testimony that he pleased God.

Enoch's life was so dedicated to God that one day God took him directly home so that he was not found. The fact that the Hebrews writer tells us he was not found means that someone looked for him and could not find him.

---

[1] George DeHoff, *DeHoff Old Testament Commentary Vol.1* (DeHoff Publications, 1976) 24.

He changed worlds without having to die. One of the more poetic descriptions which I have heard of Enoch's relationship with God says that they walked together as friends and one day God said, "We are closer to my house than yours, come home with me." I like that thought.

Will anyone else ever be translated by God? I believe that the answer is yes. Listen to **1 Corinthians 15:50-54**. The faithful who are alive at the coming of Christ will be changed to fit the heavenly home with God. That is what happened with Enoch.

We also know from scripture that Enoch was a prophet who prophesied about the coming punishment of the wicked as we see in **Jude 14,15.**

Where Abel's faith is seen in his offering, Enoch's faith is seen in his walking with God.

Questions on Enoch:

1. How is Enoch different from the Patriarchs who preceded and follow him in Genesis 5?
2. What does it mean to walk with God?
3. Is it possible to walk with God today?
4. What is unique about Enoch?
5. How many men in the Bible are said to walk with God?
6. Who should expect to be translated by God?
7. Discuss the facts about Enoch that fit the equation, "saving faith =B+T+O".

NOTES

NOAH

The next hero discussed by the Hebrews writer is Noah. Noah, along with his immediate family, survived the flood which destroyed all of the world. Noah is described as a just man, perfect in his generations (Genesis 6:9) while the world in which he lived was called wicked. When the wickedness of man caused God to regret that he had ever made man, we are told that Noah found grace in the eyes of the LORD (Genesis 6:8). Noah walked with God at a time when the world was filled with violence and was corrupt. This is the setting of our lesson. As you can see it is a lesson filled with contrasts.

Now, look at what the Hebrews writer says about this outstanding man. *"By faith Noah, being divinely warned of things not yet seen, moved with Godly fear, prepared an ark for the saving of his household, by which he condemned the world and became heir of the righteousness which is according to faith."* (Hebrews 11:7). Because of Noah's upstanding character, God warned him of the impending flood and told him to build an ark in order to save himself, his family, and a remnant of the creatures who lived upon the earth at that time.

The Hebrews writer says he was warned of things not yet seen. There had never been a global flood before. From what is written earlier in Genesis it is possible that it had not even rained before this time. **Genesis 2:5, 6.** This being true, what we read says volumes about Noah's faith. It says that even though he did not fully understand everything he was being told, he still took God at his word. He saw the seriousness of the situation and moved by godly fear, built the ark.

This was a huge undertaking. As the cubit equals approximately eighteen inches, the ark would have measured 450 feet long, 75 feet wide, and 45 feet high. It had three decks divided into compartments with a window course around the top. This "boat" was to hold Noah's family, a sample pair of every creature on the earth (seven of the clean animals), and provisions for all of them. George DeHoff suggests that the ark had as much shipping space as a freight train having 1000 cars.[2] Some have

---

[2] George DeHoff, *DeHoff Old Testament Commentary Vol.1* (DeHoff Publications, 1976) 27.

calculated that there was room in the ark for 7000 species of animal.

It could have taken as long as 100 years to build. I come up with this figure from the fact that Noah was 500 when Shem was born (Genesis 5:32) and 600 when God brought the flood (Genesis 7:11). It is possible that it could have taken less time than that because when God gave Noah the commission to build the ark he made reference to his sons and son's wives (Genesis 6:18). Noah would have had to take God seriously or been moved with godly fear to take on this gargantuan task. Because of Noah's respect for God and his fear of God's wrath, he built the ark.

Noah accepted the challenge to be different. No one else was building an ark. Even before this, he stood out from the others of his generation. Genesis says he was perfect in his generation. Don't you know this opened him up to a lot of ridicule and maybe even hatred? As a rule, men have very little respect for those who are different. Noah was different. His faith was a judgment on others. Through his obedience, Noah condemned the world.

The last thing the Hebrews writer says is that Noah was an heir of righteousness which comes through faith.

This means that because of his obedient faith, God declared him righteous.

Some lessons from Noah

(1) The need for preparation. **Matthew 24:37.** God told Noah a flood was coming. He did not say the exact time. We know Christ is coming so we must prepare ourselves to be ready.

(2) The need for obedience. **Hebrews 11:7.** Had Noah not obeyed and built the ark, he would have been destroyed with the rest of the world.

(3) The reality of salvation. **1 Peter 3:20.** Just as the waters of the flood separated Noah and his family from the wickedness and corruption of his world, so the waters of baptism separate the sinner from the wickedness and corruption of his former sin filled life. In both cases obedience was necessary to receive the salvation.

(4) The power of righteousness. **2 Peter 2:5.** Noah was spared due to his righteousness.

Questions on Noah:

1. Describe how Noah stands out from the generation of mankind in which he lived.
2. What tremendous responsibility did God give Noah to fulfill?
3. True or False. Noah fully understood God's task for him. Explain your answer.
4. In what way could Noah be considered a preacher of righteousness?
5. How did Noah condemn the world by his obedience and at the same time God condemn the world by his decision to destroy the world by the flood?
6. What does it mean to be an heir of righteousness?
7. Does the faith of Noah fit the "belief + trust + obedience" model?

NOTES

ABRAHAM

Of all the heroes of faith listed in Hebrews 11 more space is given to Abraham than any other. In verses 8-10 we see Abraham's willingness to leave his home at the command of God. Verses 11 and 12 deal with the faith of Abraham and Sarah in accepting God's promise of a son in their old age. Then verses 17-19 tell of Abraham's faith in offering Isaac. Let's examine these evidences of one man's faith.

First, there is his willingness to leave his home and familiar surroundings. *"By faith Abraham obeyed when he was called to go out to the place which he would receive as an inheritance. And he went out, not knowing where he was going. By faith he dwelt in the land of promise as in a foreign country, dwelling in tents with Isaac and Jacob, the heirs with him of the same promise; for he waited for the city which has foundations, whose builder and maker is God." (Hebrews 11:8-10).* This refers back to the passage of scripture in Genesis 12 that we call, the call of Abraham.

Genesis 12:1-4. Obedience to God here would require a great deal of trust in God. Abraham was asked to leave home and family and go out without fully knowing the destination. He was leaving an established community to wander in the wilderness of Palestine as a transient sheep herder. And bear in mind, Abraham was already 75 years old at the time he received these instructions from God. I believe that God did this in order to protect Abraham. By removing Abraham from Haran, God was removing him from a center of worship to the idol goddess Nana.[3] Removing him from Haran also removed him from the temptations and pressures of the idol worship of the city. Abraham's own father, Terah, was an idol worshipper as we read in **Joshua 24:2.** While Abraham did finally settle near Beersheba, he never was a citizen of Canaan. This land was promised to his descendants. **Genesis 12:7.** That promise was fulfilled by God bringing the Israelites into this land following the Exodus from Egypt. Abraham trusted God enough to leave home and family at the age of 75 and go to a land that would never be his, but would one day belong to his descendants, all because God told him to. That is an <u>accepting</u> faith. **Romans 4:3.**

---

[3] Charles E. Pfeiffer *Old Testament History* (Canon Press 1973) 54-55.

A second example of faith is seen in Abraham's acceptance of God's promise of a heritage. *'By faith Sarah herself also received strength to conceive seed, and she bore a child when she was past the age, because she judged him faithful who had promised. Therefore from one man, and him as good as dead, were born as many as the stars of the sky in multitude – innumerable as the sand which is by the seashore." (Hebrews 11:11,12.)* God promised Abraham that he would make of him a great nation. At the time he left Haran, he had no children and was already 75. This fact became a worry for Abraham as we see in **Genesis 15:2, 3.** God reassured Abraham that his descendants would be as numerous as the stars and the sand on the seashore. **Genesis 15:3-5.** When Abraham was 99, God sent messengers to remind Abraham of the promise that the blessing would come through a child born to him and Sarah. **Genesis 18:9-15.** Then in **Genesis 21:1-7** we read of the fulfillment of that promise. Abraham did not know how, but he knew that God had promised a heritage and God could and would deliver. At the age of 100 he held his son by Sarah, Isaac.

The third proof of Abraham's faith may be the most outstanding of them all; the offering of Isaac. *"By faith*

Abraham, when he was tested, offered up Isaac, and he who had received the promises offered up his only begotten son, of whom it was said, 'In Isaac your seed shall be called,' concluding that God was able to raise him up, even from the dead, from which he also received him in a figurative sense." (Hebrews 11:17-19). Think about this command of God and what it took for Abraham to obey. Abraham had waited 100 years for Isaac's birth. He had been assured by God that the blessing and the great nation promises would come through Isaac and not Ishmael or anyone else born in Abraham's household. Now, God is telling him to offer him as a sacrifice; to kill him. The text gives no indication of Abraham putting up any argument. Instead of arguing, Abraham took Isaac, the son of promise, to the mountain of God to sacrifice him as God had commanded. **Genesis 22:1-14.** Abraham probably did not fully understand, but he trusted God to keep his promises, so he obeyed. His faith is clearly seen in his answer to Isaac's question about the location of the animal for sacrifice in **Genesis 22:8.** The Hebrews writer described this faith in **Hebrews 11:19.**

If we were to describe Abraham's faith, we would have to say that, even though he could not see the end results of God's commands at the time, he trusted God to keep his promises and obeyed. Because of this, James would use Abraham as an example of working faith as we see in **James 2:21-23.**

Questions on Abraham:

1. How does the "evidence of things not seen" describe Abraham's faith?
2. Why is Abraham a good example of working faith?
3. Explain why Abraham might have needed reassurance concerning the seed or heritage portion of God's promise to him.
4. What about Abraham's answer to Isaac about the lamb or animal for sacrifice demonstrated his faith?
5. What is a possible reason for God to command Abraham to offer Isaac?
6. What are some examples of belief, of trust, and of obedience in Abraham's story?
7. Explain the correlation between Abraham's sacrifice of Isaac and Jesus' sacrifice.

Isaac

As Abraham was the most prominent character of the Old Testament and has the most space given to him by the writer of Hebrews, Isaac almost seems out of place. He seems to be more of an "everyman" than many of the others listed in Hebrews 11. The writer tells us, *"By faith Isaac blessed Jacob and Esau concerning things to come"* (Hebrews 11:20).

The majority of the space given to the record of Isaac's life in the scriptures has to do with his relationship to others. He comes between two dominant personalities, being the son of Abraham and the father of Jacob. He serves as a sort of transition character in the Old Testament narrative. What we know of his life is covered in a few verses spread over about five chapters. In Genesis 21, we read of his birth and childhood. In chapter 22, we read the account of Abraham's faith in the interrupted sacrifice of him to God. In chapter 24, we read of his marriage to Rebekah following the death of his mother.

If you were to make a time-line of Isaac's life it might read like this: He was born when his father was 100 years old. He married his wife, Rebekah, when he was 40. For nineteen years his marriage went childless then at the age of 60 his twin sons, Esau and Jacob, were born. The next major event of his life occurs when he is over 100 and beginning to face the end of life. At this stage he pronounces the blessing on his sons. Then Isaac died at the age of 180.

Some of the earliest evidence of Isaac's faith is seen in the events that took place on Mt. Moriah when Abraham was prepared to sacrifice him. Abraham was old, and Isaac was young. Isaac could have escaped. For that scene to happen as it did, Isaac had to submit to it. I believe that the explanation could be that Abraham told him that God would provide the animal. Isaac knew that Abraham trusted God, and he trusted his father, Abraham. So, Isaac allowed himself to be placed on the altar.

As the son of promise, he was the primary inheritor of his father's lands and possessions. **Genesis 25:5.** While Isaac was ordinary, he was greatly blessed by God. **Genesis 25:11.**

Isaac was not perfect. He made mistakes. He sinned. Among his flaws was his favoritism toward Esau.

Genesis 25:28. This could have been a contributing factor to his being deceived at the time of the giving of the blessing. He also, like his father, lied about his relationship with his wife while in a foreign territory during a time of famine. **Genesis 26:7**. This could have contributed to the disputes over wells he had with the Philistines. Even in this, Isaac tried to avoid strife. **Genesis 26:21ff**.

The scene in Isaac's life that the Hebrews writer focuses on as a proof of faith is the blessing of his sons. It was common practice for a man when he neared the end of his life to give his blessing to his sons. Usually the main blessing, or greater blessing, would go to the oldest for he would be the possessor of the birthright. In this case, Esau, the older son, had already sold his birthright to his younger brother **(Genesis 25:29-34)** so the passing of the mantel of leadership was not as clear cut. When Isaac grew older his eyesight began to fail and feeling that his time was short, decided to get on with the business of giving the blessing. Esau, the older, was his favorite, the firstborn, and the expected recipient of the father's blessing. Isaac told him to hunt and prepare savory venison the way he liked and then he would give the blessing. Rebekah heard the plan and while Esau was gone worked Jacob into the picture by dressing him in Esau's clothing and sending him in to Isaac with savory goat. Isaac was fooled and gave the blessing to Jacob. When Esau, returned all that was left was the promise that he would serve his brother. [This prophecy was completely fulfilled when the Edomites, descendants of Esau, were made servants of Israel.]

Admittedly, Isaac was tricked, but before the birth of these boys God had told Rebekah, *'two nations are in your womb, two peoples will be separated from your body; one people shall be stronger than the other, and the older shall serve the younger"* (Genesis 25:23). This event was a fulfillment of that prophecy. To Isaac's credit, even though he gave the blessing to the younger son because of trickery, he did not back down. He stated, "*I have blessed him and indeed he shall be blessed"* (Genesis 27:33). Isaac even gave further blessing to Jacob when he sent him to Padan Aram to find a wife. **Genesis 28:3, 4.**

This is all we read of Isaac until we read of his death some 63 years later in **Genesis 35:27-29.**

The writer of Hebrews tells us this blessing concerning things to come was by faith. As he had received the blessing of Abraham, he knew that his heir would have the promise as well. In all of this the promise of descendants that would be as numerous as the stars and the sand on the seashore was not realized until much later. Isaac was one and he only had two sons. This blessing was truly a confidence that God would deliver on his promise. It was the substance of things hoped for and the evidence of things not seen.

Questions on Isaac:

1. What tests of faith did Isaac face in his life?
2. How can Isaac's refusal to withdraw his blessing to Jacob be seen as a sign of faith?
3. How can the fact that Isaac was more of an "everyman" help us with our faith?
4. Explain how the blessing of his sons can be said to be by faith.
5. Is there evidence of belief, trust, and obedience in Isaac's actions?

Jacob & Joseph

The men we will study in this lesson are the last two major characters in the book of Genesis. The scenes from their lives, which the Hebrews writer has selected for his focus, occur near the end of their lives.

"*By faith Jacob, when he was dying, blessed each of the sons of Joseph, and worshipped, leaning on the top of his staff.*"

"*By faith Joseph, when he was dying, made mention of the departure of the children of Israel, and gave instructions concerning his bones.*" (Hebrews 11:21,22).

As John said at the close of his gospel account of Jesus, many other things could be written concerning Jacob and Joseph that would have demonstrated their faith, but these events are sufficient to show that these were indeed men of faith.

When we look at Jacob in this text, he is now a very old man; approximately 147 years old. He has paid several times for deceiving his father, Isaac, in the matter of the blessing. On his wedding night Jacob's father-in-law, Laban, switched brides on him, then made him work an additional seven years for Rachel to be his wife. Later on, ten of his sons would deceive him about the whereabouts of Joseph, favored son of Rachel, after they had sold him into slavery. They allowed their father to believe that Joseph had died, torn by some wild beast. Now, near the end of his life he has been reunited with the son he had thought to be dead, has seen his entire family move to Egypt where they are to be protected from the great famine, and nearing the end of life is giving out the blessings to his sons. It is at this time that he also pronounces blessings on the two sons of Joseph. The event is recorded in **Genesis 48.** The first part of this blessing is seen in the fact that Jacob adopted Joseph's sons as his own. **Genesis 48:3-5.** From this point on, instead of reading of the tribe of Joseph, we will read of the tribes of Ephraim and Manasseh. This also means that Joseph's family will receive one portion more than any of the other families. As it turns out, this works out well because God will take the tribe of Levi for his own in the place of the redeemed, dedicated firstborn of the other families. We read of that in **Numbers 3:12.**

The actual blessing of Joseph's sons is recorded in **Genesis 48:14-16.** At this time Jacob blesses the younger son over the older. He said that they would be a part of the promised blessing which had passed through Abraham, Isaac, and Jacob; that they would grow into a multitude in the midst of the earth. [I find it interesting here that Jacob, the younger son who stole the blessing from his older brother, blesses Ephraim, the younger, over Manasseh, the older son.] As we study on through the Old Testament, we will see that Ephraim truly does become the prominent tribe of the Northern kingdom as Judah is in the Southern kingdom. Jacob would not live to see this but, by faith, he blessed these boys in this way.

Concerning Joseph, the Hebrews writer says that he made mention of the departure of Israel from Egypt and gave instructions about his bones. Prior to his death, Jacob had already made Joseph promise to bury him with his fathers back in Palestine (Genesis 47:29-31), which he did. Following the burial, all of Jacob's family pretty well settled themselves in Egypt in the land of Goshen. As Joseph neared the end of his 110-year life, he told his brothers that God would surely visit them and take them to the land he had promised Abraham, Isaac, and Jacob. He then said, "when you go, take my bones with you." The instructions are given in **Genesis 50:24-26.** The fulfillment is recorded in **Exodus 13:19.** Consider these instructions. Joseph knew the promise which had been made to his forefathers. He knew, from earlier experience, God to be a God who provides and who keeps his promises. This being true, the land would be given to Abraham and Isaac's descendants some time. When that time came he wanted his bones carried back for burial. All told, the Israelites would be in the land of Egypt 430 years. What Joseph is requesting might not happen for another 300 years. Truly this demonstrates a great faith in God.

Questions on *Jacob and Joseph:*

1. What do the hardships endured by Jacob while in the home of Laban say about his faith?
2. How does Jacob's blessing of Joseph's sons tie them to God's promised blessing to Abraham, Isaac, and Jacob?
3. Is there any significance to Jacob's blessing the younger son over the older? Explain.
4. How does Jacob's blessing reveal his confidence and trust in God?
5. What experiences did Joseph have that would cause him to trust God?
6. What promise to Abraham was Joseph depending on by giving instructions concerning his bones?
7. Discuss how Joseph's understanding of God's providence would serve as the foundation for his request of his brothers.

NOTES

MOSES

Moses is one of the few Bible characters whose whole life is recorded. We know some of the situation in Egypt at the time of his birth. We know that the first 40 years of his life were spent in Egypt as the son of Pharaoh's daughter. The second 40 years of his life were spent as a herdsman in the land of Midian. And the final 40 years of his life were spent leading God's people back to the land promised to Abraham, Isaac, and Jacob by God. We know that at the end of his life he was allowed to view that land of promise from Mt. Pisgah before his death and that he was buried by God.

The verses we will examine from Hebrews 11 make reference to all of these different stages in the life of this man chosen by God to lead his people.

"By faith Moses, when he was born, was hidden three months by his parents because they saw he was a beautiful child; and they were not afraid of the king's command. By faith Moses, when he became of age, refused to be called

the son of Pharaoh's daughter, choosing rather to suffer affliction with the people of God than to enjoy the passing pleasures of sin, esteeming the reproach of Christ greater riches than the treasures in Egypt; for he looked to the reward. By faith he forsook Egypt, not fearing the wrath of the king; for he endured as seeing Him who is invisible. By faith he kept the Passover and the sprinkling of blood lest he who destroyed the firstborn should touch them. By faith they passed through the Red Sea as by dry land, whereas the Egyptians, attempting to do so, were drowned." (Hebrews 11:23-29)

In these verses the writer looks at Moses' faith at five stages in his life.

The first stage has more to do with Moses' parents, Amram and Jochebed, than with Moses, himself. Having parents who demonstrated such outstanding faith was surely a factor in Moses becoming a man of faith. The king's decree was that all boy babies born to the Israelites were to be thrown into the river. These parents hid their newborn son three months in order to avoid sending him to certain death in the Nile. It was only when they could hide him no longer that they made a waterproof basket or ark and placed the baby into it as they put him in the river.

Think about the faith necessary to defy a king's decree. Babies make noise. I wonder how they were able to hide him for three months. Then there was the faith demonstrated in the making of the bull rush ark to protect the baby while he was in the river. They did not know for sure what the reaction would be when Pharaoh's daughter found their baby. Because of this faithful action, Jochebed was allowed to nurse her son and take part in his early training. Surely this early training by this woman of faith played a great role in the actions and decisions of Moses when he grew older.

Some of those decisions are discussed in verses 24 through 26 of our text. Even though he had been raised in the palace of the king, he knew that his people were oppressed. He chose to stand up for his people. This led to the killing of an Egyptian taskmaster and Moses' eventual fugitive exile from Egypt. **Exodus 2:11-15.** The Hebrews writer says that "...he *esteemed the reproach of Christ greater riches than the treasures of Egypt."* What do you suppose is meant by this phrase, "the reproach of Christ"? I would suggest that he accepted the same kind of reproach and rejection that Christ suffered. Isaiah described Christ's reproach in **Isaiah 53:3.** Moses, as the result of his actions in standing up and defending his fellow Israelite, found himself despised and rejected by both Israelite and Egyptian.

Moses had the faith and courage to set out into the unknown (v.27). All of his life up to this point had been spent in Egypt; most of it in Pharaoh's palace. Now, he finds himself living in Midian and caring for the flocks of his father-in-law, Jethro. For the next 40 years he will learn the ways of the wilderness in preparation for going back into Egypt and leading God's people out. During this time an even crueler ruler would arise in Egypt. At the end of this time, God will give Moses his commission to go and demand that his people be released. By this stage in his life, he has had 40 years training in Egypt followed by 40 years of training in Midian. He is now ready to carry out God's plan.

Verse 28 of the text points to the obedience of Moses' faith. God was bringing the plagues on Egypt. As a result, the nation had just about been brought to its knees through the loss of livestock and all crops, coupled with physical illness. Now, God is ready to bring his final punch, the death of the firstborn. This is the first time the Israelites will be required to do anything in regard to the plagues. Now, they are to prepare the Passover lamb, sprinkle its blood on their doorposts showing that death had already entered that house, and eat the Passover meal fully dressed and ready to leave. In all of the country of Egypt, all who failed to sprinkle the blood experienced the death of the firstborn in their house. Nothing like this had happened before. The Israelites had not been required to do anything to avoid any of the previous plagues other than to stay in Goshen. Now, they are told to perform the curious act of putting lamb's blood around their doors. True faith requires complete obedience.

Then there is the crossing of the Red Sea on dry land (v.29). It took faith to step out and cross. You would have to trust God to hold back the waters until you could get across. Not only were these Israelites able to get across safely, they were also able to witness the drowning of the Egyptian forces that were pursuing them. This was one more demonstration of God's power and providential care. Still, to cross safely out of Egypt, these people had to trust and obey.

Questions on Moses:

1. Discuss the idea that children's faith is dependent on the faith of the parents.
2. How might Moses' belief and trust in God have been weakened by his exile from Egypt?
3. What is meant by the reproach of Christ?
4. Explain how Moses' forty years in Midian may have
5. How is the crossing of the Red Sea a demonstration of belief, trust, and obedience?

THE FALL OF JERICHO AND RAHAB

In this lesson we will depart somewhat from the format we have been using in previous lessons. In verses 30 and 31 of the eleventh chapter of Hebrews the author refers to two events that happened at about the same time. They are the destruction of Jericho and the salvation of Rahab and her family.

"By faith the walls of Jericho fell down after they were encircled for seven days. By faith the harlot Rahab did not perish with those who did not believe, when she had received the spies with peace." (Hebrews 11:30,31).

The first of these events is a clear example of trusting, obedient fait

The Israelites had witnessed once again the awesome power of God as they had been able to cross the Jordan River on dry land even though it was the Spring of the year and the river was flooding out of its banks. At the command of God, they had carried out twelve stones from the riverbed and erected a monument at Gilgal as a reminder of God's deliverance. Now, they are approaching the walled city of Jericho. God gave specific instructions on how they were to conquer this city. God told them to march around the city in silence once a day for six days.

On the seventh day they were to march around the city seven times and following the seventh orbit they were to shout and God would cause the city walls to fall (Joshua 6:1-20). For six days the army of Israel, divided into two groups with the priests in the center, marched once around the city then returned to camp. On the seventh day they got an earlier start, made seven trips around the city, shouted, and God caused the walls to fall. For six days the only sound heard from the army of Israel was the sound of the ram's horns blown by the priests. Faith is clearly evident in these actions.

To the best of my knowledge there is not a single manual on warfare that recommends defeating an enemy by marching around his encampment for seven days. There could be no doubt, when the battle was won and the city taken, that it was because of the hand of God. There is no other explanation. Still, this great victory would not have happened were it not for the obedience of the Israelite army.

God required that the Israelites defeat and drive out the Canaanites as they took possession of the land because these people were known for idolatry and the rejection of God. The Hebrews writer says they did not believe. If they were allowed to remain in the land they could and would have turned the hearts of Israel away from God. That is what we have recorded in the book of Judges and see in the life of Solomon who married many foreign wives (1 Kings 11:1-10).

This brings us to the faith of Rahab. Rahab was a citizen of the doomed city. She was a harlot. She is also a demonstration of an unprecedented faith which led to the saving of her whole family. She hid and protected the men sent to spy out the city. She wanted to be a part of this people who had been protected by God. (See **James 2:25** and **Joshua chapters 2 and 6**.)

Rahab's faith was a triumph over practically everything in her life. It was a triumph over sin, her occupation being one that would not predispose her to righteousness. It was a triumph over patriotism. Her own city and race were rejected by her decision. It was a triumph over the fear of death. She could have been killed by her own people if her act of hiding the spies had been discovered or she could die with her city when God brought the destruction. It was a triumph over <u>unpopularity</u>. There was no love between Israel and the inhabitants of Jericho. Her faith was a triumph over <u>meager information</u>. All she knew about the God of Israel she had learned by rumor. Her faith was a triumph over <u>the religious convictions of her loved ones</u>. The whole city was marked for destruction. Her faith was a triumph over <u>wild alarm</u>. In order to be saved from the destruction of their city, Rahab and her family had to remain in her house. This must have been difficult and required much faith because her house was on a wall and the walls of the city were falling down.

Rahab's faith was <u>stable</u>. She did not waver during the six days Israel was marching around the city with no apparent result. Her faith was <u>evangelistic</u>. She was able to save her family. Her faith was <u>redemptive</u>. She went from the life of a harlot to be the wife of an Israelite and in the lineage of Christ (Matthew 1:5). Her faith was also <u>sacrificial</u> in that she gave up everything she had in Jericho in order to cast her lot with the people of God.

[I find a parallel between her putting a red cord in her window and staying in her house during the destruction of Jericho and what happened in Egypt when the Israelites were to put blood on their doorposts and remain in their houses while the death angel passed over Egypt. Both are evidence of faith.]

Questions on the fall of Jericho and Rahab:

1. What events could have served as a basis of faith for the Israelites at Gilgal?
2. Explain how the statement, "God gave the victory", fit the events at Jericho.
3. What part did faith play in the victory over Jericho?
4. Discuss how the statement, "saving faith is made up of belief, trust, and obedience", fit this event.
5. Why did God command the Canaanites be driven from the land?
6. List some of the challenges Rahab faced because of her faith.
7. Which act was the greater evidence of Rahab's faith; the hiding of the spies, the placing of the cord in her window, or remaining in her house during the fall of the city? Explain your answer.
8. Describe Rahab's faith.

GIDEON

The man we will study in this lesson might not, at first glance, fit the usual idea of a hero. When we first meet him, he is hiding in a wine press threshing wheat. One reason we might enjoy studying Gideon might be that he stands out as an ordinary man who had to deal with doubts. In spite of this, the Hebrews writer includes him in this listing of examples of faith. *"And what more shall I say? For the time would fail me to tell of Gideon and Barak and Samson and Jephthah, also of David and Samuel and the prophets:"* (Hebrews 11:32).

Gideon was one of the men who served as a judge over the people of Israel during the time between the conquering of the land and the anointing of Saul as the first king. These judges were military commanders and governing authorities as well as judges over disputes among the people. Often, they were called directly by God to fill this role and during the reign of the judge the people usually stayed close to God in their devotion and enjoyed peace. When the judge died, though, the people usually reverted to following the pagan gods of the land and God would again allow them to be oppressed by their neighbors. At the time we meet Gideon, Israel has been oppressed by Midian and their allies for seven years. This oppression was severe. The Midianites were starving Israel, keeping them poor and weak. **Judges 6:2-6.** This situation explains why Gideon was in the wine press threshing his wheat (Judges 6:11).

Apparently, God saw something in Gideon that is not readily visible to us. The angel called him a mighty man of valor (v.12). One key is the fact that God was with Gideon. Gideon needed convincing. **Judges 6:12-18.** At this point God gives the first of several reassuring signs to this questioning man (v.21).

Now, God has Gideon's attention and gives him a mission to perform. He is to tear down the local altar to Baal and replace it with an altar to God. Gideon waited until after dark, then did the LORD's bidding. When the men of Ophrah came after Gideon for destroying the Baal altar, Gideon's father spoke up and said, "let Baal plead for himself." In this way God protected Gideon and strengthened him for the major task of leading Israel against the host of Midian.

Gideon still needed assurance, so we see the tests of the fleece in **Judges 6:36-40.** Please notice the patience of God in his dealings with Gideon. Time and time again God gives him signs that he is the man for the job and that God will be there to aid him.

This brings us to God's troop reduction program. God wants these people to realize that it is He who is giving them this victory over their enemy. Thirty-two thousand answered Gideon's call for soldiers. Although this might sound like a large army, it is nothing in comparison to the size of the host they are about to face (7:12). Even at that, God told Gideon he had too many men. The first reduction then came when all who were fearful or afraid were sent home. Twenty-two thousand left. This left a force of one thousand which God said was still too large. The remaining group was taken to the river where they were watched as they drank. Three hundred who got down and lapped like a dog were kept and the rest were sent home.

Gideon now has an army of three hundred to go against the Midian multitude and God assures him once more that He is with them (Judges 7:9-15).

This brings us to the battle. Gideon's three hundred are all armed with a trumpet and a pitcher with a torch inside it. Picture the scene. In one hand they have their trumpet and in the other they have the torch. Where is the sword or bow or any other offensive weapon? God had it (v.20). Gideon divided his troop into three groups and arranged them on three sides of the enemy camp. On Gideon's signal they broke the pitchers, blew the trumpets, and cried out, "the sword of the LORD and of Gideon." **Judges 7:21, 22.**

What made this weak, often questioning man a hero of faith? Although he was sometimes doubting, when he acted it was because of his trust in God. You do not tear down people's places of worship to false gods unless you really believe God is with you. One normally would not go to battle against a large, well-armed force with three hundred poorly armed men unless you trust God to give the victory. Gideon went up against the force of Midian with men armed only with trumpets and torches. God can take doubting men and make them mighty men of valor.

Questions on Gideon:

1. Based on Hebrews 11:6, could you conclude that Gideon had pleasing faith when he was approached by God's messenger?
2. What was the key to Gideon's successes?
3. How does the account of Gideon's life prove that God is longsuffering?
4. Describe the armature used by Gideon's army in the battle with Midian.
5. Explain how the troop reduction and armaments used in the battle prove Gideon's faith.
6. What steps did God take to prove his presence with Gideon?

NOTES

BARAK

As we continue in our study of the men and women of faith listed in Hebrews chapter 11 you may have noticed that some of these individuals seem to demonstrate a greater level of faith than others. A case in point are the Judges listed in verse 32 of the text. *"And what more shall I say? For the time would fail me to tell of Gideon and Barak and Samson and Jephthah, also of David and Samuel and the prophets:" (Hebrews 11:32).* If you have devoted much time to a study of the Judges then you probably noticed that for the most part these God-chosen leaders were flawed individuals. That was the case with Gideon. It is also an accurate description of Barak, whom we will study in this lesson. It will also be true of Jephthah and Samson, heroes we will study in upcoming lessons. Since these men have such obvious character flaws we might wonder how they could be listed in the same grouping with men like Abraham and Moses. I believe that as we study the actions of these men you will find that like

Abraham, who lied about Sarah, and Moses who tried to make excuses to God, that these men demonstrated lives of faith in spite of the flaws in their character and that should be a great encouragement to each of us. Let's look at Barak.

Besides his mention in Hebrews 11, Barak is only mentioned in Judges four and five: two chapters which describe the same series of events. Barak is the man chosen by God to lead the armies of Israel as they threw off the oppression of Jabin, King of Canaan. For twenty years God had allowed Jabin to punish Israel for their idolatrous rebellion. Now, that they have been awakened to their failure by this oppression and, due to their repentance, God is going to remove this yoke of oppression.

This takes place during the time that Deborah, the prophetess, is serving as judge in the area inhabited by the tribes of Zebulon, Issachar, and Naphtali. It is she who informs Barak of God's intention that he lead the army of Israel as they went up against the army of Jabin which was led by his commander, Sisera. This would be a daunting task. The Canaanite army was highly mobile. Jabin had 900 iron chariots.

Still, God had chosen Barak to lead an army of ten thousand from Naphtali and Zebulon into battle. In addition to allowing him this large army, God had also promised to go before the army and deliver Sisera and the army of Canaan into Barak's hands. One might have expected Barak to immediately go to the battle with this kind of incentive. Instead, he refused to go unless Deborah, the judge and prophetess went as well. We are not told why Barak made this stipulation. Perhaps he believed that he would have a greater chance for victory if God's prophet were present. No matter what his reasoning, because he made this stipulation, he was told that the glory for the victory would not be his but would go to a woman. **Judges 4:9.**

To prepare for the battle, Israel's troops were called together at Kedesh of Naphtali. From there they traveled to Mt. Tabor, which overlooks the Valley of Jezreel, an area which was the scene of many Old Testament battles. When Sisera learned that the army of Israel was gathered on Mt. Tabor he moved his forces to the Kishon river, which was located across the Jezreel valley from Mt. Tabor. This would make sense since his was a chariot army and chariots do not move well in the mountains.

As God had promised, he went before the army of Israel and defeated Sisera's force, (possibly by the use of a flash flood on the river (**Judges 5:21**)). God made it possible for the army of Israel to completely rout the Canaanite troop.

As promised Barak did not receive any glory from the great victory. In the heat of retreat, Sisera left his chariot and traveled on foot to the tent of Heber the Kennite. Heber's wife, Jael, hid Sisera, demonstrated hospitality in giving him milk, and killed him by driving a tent stake through his head as he slept. **Judges 4:17-21**. The glory and praise went to Jael for her part in the defeat Canaan's army, Israel's enemy.

How did Barak show himself to be a hero of faith? His request that Deborah accompany him might seem to be a sign of a lack of faith. Perhaps the Hebrews writer's explanation might help us to understand Barak's inclusion in this chapter. He was part of a group of whom the writer said, *"through faith subdued kingdoms, worked righteousness, obtained promises, stopped the mouths of lions..." (Hebrews 11:33)*. By his actions Barak did have a part in subduing kingdoms and he definitely obtained promises. He, like Gideon, was outnumbered and out armed. Still he was able to win the victory when he obeyed the command of God. He obeyed, and his obedience demonstrated his faith and trust in God. It takes trust to obey.

Questions on Barak:

1. What action might cause us to overlook Barak as a man of faith?
2. How can studying flawed, weak humans aid us in our faith?
3. How did God show Barak that He (God) is worthy of trust?
4. Explain how Barak was a hero of faith in spite of his request that Deborah accompany him.
5. How does Hebrews 11:33 prove that Barak belongs on this list of heroes?
6. Are belief, trust, and obedience visible in Barak's actions? In what way?
7. Discuss how the promise that the glory for the victory would go to a woman might make Barak a lesser known person of faith.

SAMSON

If you were asked to make a list of men and women of faith in the Bible, the man we will study in this lesson might not make your top twenty. Although he is famous for many things, most of us do not look to him as an example of faith. If you were to mention Samson to the average person you would most likely hear comments on his hair or his great strength. These are the things people remember about Samson. In some ways this is surprising because the strength that enabled him to perform his mighty feats and defeat Philistines by the thousands wasn't even his own strength. He did those things by the power of God. That is what we read in **Judges 14:6,19; 15:14; and 16:20,28.**

If we were called upon to come up with a descriptive phrase for Samson it would probably be something along the line of lust-filled hothead. Just a quick look at Samson's life reveals a man who was always with a Philistine woman and was subject to fits of temper. What we may fail to realize is these temper fits and associations with Philistine women were part of God's plan to punish the Philistines. Look at **Judges 14:4.**

Samson is one of just a handful of men to have their birth proclaimed by God through one of his messengers. That announcement is found in **Judges 13:3-5.** Samson was not only promised by God, he was also to be dedicated to God his entire life. That was the case with the Nazarite. During the period of his vow, the Nazarite lived a life of dedicated service to God. The rules for the Nazarite vow are given in **Numbers 6:2-8.** We notice three main rules. The first was the Nazarite did not cut his hair during the period of his vow. This vow could vary in length depending on the individual. The second was he was not to partake of wine or anything from the grapevine. The third rule was that the Nazarite was not to go near any dead bodies during his vow. Looking at Samson's life we would have to assume that his vow was a modified version of the general Nazarite vow for the only one of these rules that was enforced his whole life was the "hair rule". We can come to this conclusion because he was always around dead bodies and he certainly ate and drank at his marriage feast.

Samson's dedication to God's service began before he was born. In preparation for his life of service, his mother was told to drink no wine or eat anything unclean during her pregnancy.

Looking at Samson's life, it is obvious that he was a mighty tool which God used to afflict the Philistines. But, how could he be considered a man of faith? Let's examine his actions for a minute. If Samson had taken the credit for his accomplishments, we would have to say that he did not operate by faith in God. Was that the case? Did Samson think he was able to do these things by his own power? No, Samson knew that God was the source of his great strength.

I base that conclusion on two events. The first is the scene where he lost his strength. After teasing and mocking Delilah with his answers of the bowstrings, the new ropes, and the weaving his hair in the loom, he was finally pestered by her to the point he told her the truth. Look at what he attributed his strength. **Judges 16:17.** He knew that when he cut his hair the vow would be brought to an end and God would no longer be strengthening him. This tells me that he knew his mission for God and trusted God to enable him to carry out that mission.

The second event which points to Samson's trust in God took place at the end of his life when he was being used as entertainment for the Philistines. **Judges 16:28-30.** Samson placed his trust in God and was able to kill more Philistines with his death than he had killed during his life. His faith is seen in the fact that he asked and then acted. His was a "mountain moving", or maybe we should say "temple destroying" faith.

Questions on Samson:

1. How would Samson's mother not drinking wine or eating anything unclean prepare him for service to God?
2. In what ways did Samson begin to deliver Israel out of the hands of the Philistines?
3. How did Samson's life fulfill the prophecy that he would begin to deliver Israel?
4. Could Samson's allowing himself to be bound and his teasing of Delilah be seen as testing or proving God? Explain.
5. Defend the statement, "Samson is an illustration of faith motivated repentance."
6. Explain how Samson's final prayer proved his faith.
7. How do Samson's mighty deeds demonstrate his faith?

NOTES

JEPHTHAH

One truth that that has been apparent in just about every one of the heroes we have studied is that none of them were perfect. None of them were supermen with strengths and abilities far above those of mortal man. Every one of these individuals were normal human beings and so were subject to making poor choices from time to time. Every one of them had their weakness. The man we will study in this lesson is no exception.

Before we look at the man, let's first look at the background and conditions in Israel when he came to prominence. As has been the case with others who lived during the time of the judges, when Jephthah comes to our attention Israel is being oppressed by nations around them whom they should have driven out of the land when they took possession. The reason for this particular oppression is recorded in **Judges 10:6, 10-14.**

As the result of this rebellion, God has again turned them over to the bordering nations. On this occasion the oppressing people were Ammonites and Philistines; primarily Ammonites who were descendants of Lot. The Ammonites lived on the East side of the Jordan river in an area North of the lands possessed by Reuben, Gad, and half of Manasseh. These Ammonites began by oppressing the tribes dwelling East of the Jordan, but now have crossed over to afflict Judah, Benjamin, and Ephraim as well.

As at other times, the persecuted Israelites repented of their rebellion (**Judges 10:16**) and God, in his great mercy, once again brought deliverance through the leadership of a human judge. On this occasion, the delivering commander was a man named Jephthah. Jephthah, we learn, is a son of Gilead who has been driven out by his family because he is only a half-brother. **Judges 11:1-3.** In the meantime, he has been living in the land of Tob, an area East of the Jordan probably outside the borders of Israel, with his band of marauders. Naturally, when it comes time to find a leader with fighting experience to throw off the Ammonite oppression, the leaders of Gilead automatically think of their brother, Jephthah. As might be expected, before Jephthah agrees to take on this task he needs some assurances and sets some stipulations. **Judges 11:9, 10.**

When he begins the task of relieving the oppression, Jephthah first tries diplomacy. He tries to reason with the Ammonites and avoid war. First, he asks what these people have against him and his people. It always helps to know what you are fighting about. The Ammonite claim is that when Israel first moved into the area, they had taken land they had no right to; land owned by Ammon. At this stage Jephthah recounts the history of the conquest to show that the land Israel had taken did not belong to the Ammonites and on top of that, this was land given to them by God. Jephthah's argument was, "We have settled in the land our God gave us, wouldn't you do the same?" (**Judges 11:24**) Jephthah knew his history. He knew how God had led Israel in the past. When it became clear that war could not be avoided, Jephthah gathered his army and sought God's help. He even vowed to make sacrifices to God if God would give the victory. The God whom he trusted delivered Ammon into his hands (**Judges 11:32, 33**).

We would be negligent if we studied Jephthah and ignored his vow. Let's begin by asking a series of questions and allow the scriptures to answer them. (1) What exactly was Jephthah's vow? The answer is seen in **Judges 11:30, 31.** (2) Did God give the victory? Look at **Judges 11:32.**

(3) What was Jephthah's response? **Judges 11:35, 39.** Whether Jephthah actually offered his daughter as a burnt offering or merely redeemed her and dedicated her to celibacy and service to God for the remainder of her life as some students believe, the fact remains that this was Jephthah's only child. His lineage would end with her. More important than the way he fulfilled his vow is his attitude toward this vow. He recognized that a vow to God had to be taken seriously and carried it out. Notice, please, that Jephthah's daughter had the same respect for vows.

It should be obvious that Jephthah had faith in God. He acted like one who believes God exists and rewards those who diligently seek him (Hebrews 11:6). Jephthah respected the teachings of God as is seen in his knowledge of God's past dealings with His people. And he trained his daughter to have a similar respect for God. All of this points to Jephthah as a man of faith.

Questions on Jephthah:

1. How does Jephthah's account of the conquest demonstrate his faith in God?
2. Explain how the argument that God gave the disputed land to Israel when He gave the victory was a good argument to use in Jephthah's arguments to the Ammonites.
3. Was it necessary for Jephthah to make a vow to God for God to give him the victory? Explain.
4. Show how Jephthah's attitude toward his vow is a strong example of faith.
5. Discuss how Jephthah's daughter's response upon hearing of the vow is also a great demonstration of faith.
6. Should all vows before God be taken seriously? Why?

NOTES

DAVID

"And what more shall I say? For the time would fail me to tell of Gideon and Barak and Samson and Jephthah, also of David and Samuel and the prophets" (Hebrews 11:32).

When we look at David as a man of faith there are many places for us to look in the scriptures. It has been said that there is more written about David than any other Old Testament character other than Moses and Abraham. David comes from a long line of faith when you realize that his great-grandparents were Boaz and Ruth and his great-great-grandparents were Salmon and Rahab from Jericho. David did have a heritage of faith.

One of the first places we see David's faith in God voiced and displayed is at the battle sight in the valley of Elah where the forces of Israel were being taunted and challenged by the giant, Goliath of Gath. David was present to hear the giant's challenge because he had brought supplies to three of his older brothers who were in Saul's army. David's first response upon hearing the challenge says a great deal about the strength of his faith. **1 Samuel 17:26.** To David, for this man to defy Israel was for him to defy God. David had had enough experience with God's providential care to believe that he could stand up to the giant even though he, himself, was only a youth. **1 Samuel 17:33-37.** David had seen first-hand what God could do. With this knowledge and faith filled confidence David was able to face Goliath and defeat him all the while giving God credit for the victory. **1 Samuel 17:45-47.**

Sometimes the best way to know the thinking of a man is to read his writings. David is no exception. Being a shepherd, David had time to look up at the wonders of God as seen in his creation. So, he wrote **Psalm 104** as one of several songs that reveal his awe at the constant wonders of God. [See also **Psalms 8 and 19.**] David's sense of God's abiding presence and nearness is seen in his words recorded in **Psalm 139:1-12.** This knowledge enabled David to find strength when times were at their worst as we see in his actions recorded in **1 Samuel 30:1-6.** Because of his faith and trust in God at this point in his life, David was able to go on to win a great victory with God's help. Perhaps Peter had this incident in mind when he advised the persecuted Christians of his day in **1 Peter 5:6, 7.**

As has been the case with others of the heroes we have studied, David was far from a perfect individual. As the result of his sin with Bathsheba which in turn led to the murder of her husband, David would lose at least four sons. He would see a daughter raped by her brother. He would have two sons try to usurp his throne and he would lose a friend and advisor in Ahithophel. These were just a few of the consequences David faced because of his sin. When Absalom tried to take over, David was even driven from his city, Jerusalem, the city of David. Even at this low point, David's faith was still intact. Listen to his words to the priests when they tried to bring the ark of the covenant and join David in his retreat from the city. **2 Samuel 15:25-26.** It is thought by some that David wrote Psalm 3 at this time in his life. A good psalm to read to get a picture of David's faith in all the ups and downs in his life is **Psalm 27.**

As David neared the close of his life and was passing the kingdom on to his son, Solomon, we again are able to see evidence of his faith in God. Listen to his advice to his son. **1 Kings 2:3,4.**

David was known as a man after God's own heart. Through all of his life he kept his soul tender and lived with a desire to please God with his life. As a result, every king that came after him all the way up to the time of the captivities of Israel and Judah had his life and reign compared to that of David. Because of his continual trust in God and his willingness to repent in times of failure, David was the greatest earthly king Israel would ever know. One more scripture that demonstrates David's attitude toward God is seen in **2 Samuel 24:21-25.** Truly, David stands as a hero of faith.

Questions on David:

1. How might David's heritage of faith have caused him to give God the credit for his victories?
2. How does the fact that more is written about David than any other Old Testament individual, with the exception of Moses and Abraham, point to his being a man of faith?
3. What evidence is there that David was a man after God's own heart?
4. Considering the adversity David experienced in his life, should it be considered strange that he did not accuse God? Explain.
5. Might David's joining the Philistines to escape Saul's pursuit be seen as a failure of faith? How?
6. What are some examples of God's providential care toward David?
7. Give proof of belief, trust, and obedience in the life of David.

NOTES

SAMUEL

The man we study in this lesson is the last individual mentioned by name in Hebrews chapter 11. Samuel was the final judge to lead Israel prior to the time of the kings. As we examine his life we will see him filling several different roles of service to God and his people. Samuel was a priest who served in the Tabernacle and offered sacrifices. As we have mentioned, he was a judge over Israel with all of the responsibilities that went with that job. Samuel was a seer or prophet of God. And during the latter part of his life, Samuel served as advisor to both King Saul and King David.

Samuel's birth, like Samson's before him, was an answer to prayer and was announced beforehand. With Samson, the angel of God came to Manoah and his wife to announce the upcoming birth and to instruct those future parents on how they were to prepare for his birth. In the case of Samuel, his mother, Hannah, had been unable to have children and prayed fervently, asking God for a son.

She even promised to dedicate that son to God if God would only grant her request. Eli, the priest, at first rebuked Hannah for being drunk at the feast but, when he learned the reason for her distress, he promised her that God would give her the son she so desperately wanted. Samuel's birth was truly an answered prayer. **1 Samuel 1:17, 27, 28.** From reading the text it is clear that Hannah kept her promise and devoted Samuel to the service of God all of his life. From the evidence of the various jobs he filled, it is obvious that this is exactly what he did. Samuel's dedication to God is also seen in the fact that he was a Nazarite. **1 Samuel 1:11.** [See Samson for further information of the Nazarite vow.] Samuel ministered before the LORD from his youth. **1 Samuel 3:1.**

A hint of Samuel's attitude toward God is seen in that time in the history of Israel when the word of the LORD was rare and there was no widespread revelation from God, God spoke to and through Samuel. Remember, this was the time of the Judges when there was no king and everyman did what was right in his own sight. This might explain the scarcity of messages from God.

It was Samuel who successfully called the people away from their idol worship and back to the worship of

God. **1 Samuel 7:3-6.** Unlike some of the other judges who dealt only with a small portion of Israel, Samuel judged all of Israel and traveled a circuit of several of the towns. **1 Samuel 3:15-17.**

Samuel was so devoted to God that he was severely distressed when the people asked for a king (8:6). God reassured him and told him to give the people what they asked. After warning Israel what having an earthly king would entail, he gave in to their wishes and anointed God's first choice; a tall, humble man from Benjamin named Saul. Following Saul's anointing, Samuel, in what amounted to his farewell address as leader over Israel, asked for the witness of the people. **1 Samuel 12:3-5.** Following this, he challenged the people to faithfully serve God, **vs. 13-15,** and then made one last promise to encourage them to choose to serve God. **vs. 20-25.** Notice he even promised to continue to pray for them in verse 23.

Even after he stepped down as the primary leader, Samuel continued to serve as prophet and priest. He rebuked Saul for presuming to perform the duty of offering sacrifices when he did not have that right. Later it would be Samuel's sad duty to inform Saul that since he had seen fit to disregard God's commands concerning the destruction of the Amalekites that God had removed him from being King. At God's bidding, Samuel anointed the man who would be Israel's second King; the young man, David. Samuel would then serve as advisor and mentor to David. This was the case during the time that Saul began pursuing David to take his life. The last we hear of Samuel is in the strange scene where God allowed Samuel's spirit to be summoned so that he could announce Saul's doom. **1 Samuel 28:15-19.**

The life of Samuel is truly an example of a man devoted to the service of God all of his life. Really the only negative we read concerning him was that his sons did not walk in his ways. All else points to Samuel as a man who trusted God and obeyed him in all things.

Questions on Samuel:

1. What aspects of Samuel's background could have contributed to his life of faith?
2. What challenges of Samuel's life could have weakened his faith?
3. How is Samuel's distress over the people's call for a king evidence of faith?
4. Would witnessing the punishment of God against Eli's house serve to strengthen or weaken the faith of the young Samuel? Explain.
5. How does the life of Samuel compare to the other examples of faith we have studied?
6. Give accounts that point to belief, trust, and obedience in the life of Samuel

NOTES

NOTES

www.ingramcontent.com/pod-product-compliance
Lightning Source LLC
Chambersburg PA
CBHW060848050426
42453CB00008B/886